The Embrocraft A-Z of Sewing

By TREV HUNT

DEDICATION

This book is dedicated to you the reader.

CONTENTS

ACKNOWLEDGMENTS

This book is dedicated to you the reader.

INTRODUCTION

This book is one of three books on Sewing, Fabric and Embroidery terms. This particular book does not pretend to be anything more than a structured compellation of information about Sewing terms and the meaning of those terms. There's no real need for a big introduction. If you wish to learn more about Sewing related terms, you will find the book an invaluable resource. The contents of this book will feel very much like a dictionary of terms, which was exactly my intention. Please view it as one of those handy research tools that you will come back to time and again.

SEWING TERMS BEGINNING WITH

A

Acorn: A decorative brass or wooden "handle" which covers the knotted cord ends of a blind.

Air Jet Yarn: A type of open-end spinning that uses a stationary tube in which jets of air are directed to cause fibers to twist thereby forming a yarn. This process definitely influences the soft hand feel of the fabric while maintaining excellent resistance to pilling.

Alphabets: Machines with an alphabet will sew lettering stitches on to craft projects, and are often used for sewing your name onto quilts or labelling clothes. The size of the lettering and choice of font will vary depending on the make and model machine.

All-Weather Microfiber: Fabric that is tightly woven from an extremely fine poly thread with a sueded finish for a luxuriously supple feel. When combined with waterproof coating and full seam sealing, microfiber is 100% waterproof. 100% polyester.

Alter: Term used to change or revise a pattern or garment to fit an individual.

Antimicrobial: A term used for a garment that is able to resist, either naturally or chemically, the effects of microbial secretions put off by the human body, resisting odor and increasing garment life.

Anti-Pill Finish: A treatment applied to garments primarily to resist the formation of little balls on the fabric's surface due to abrasion during wear.

Appliqué: Decoration or trimming cut from one

fabric piece and stitched to another to add dimension.

Arc Rating: A value of the energy necessary to pass through any given fabric to cause with 50% probability a second- or third-degree burn. This value is measured in calories/cm2. Simply put, the Arc rating determines the protective characteristics of the fabric. The higher the Arc rating value, the greater the protection.

Armhole: Dressmaking term for where the sleeve is attached.

Arm Scye: The arm hole of a garment, where the sleeve is attached.

Arrowhead Stitch: A small triangular stitch used on a seam to add strength at points of strain.

Articulation: A design detail usually in the shoulders, elbows or knees where limbs bend to increase mobility for greater ease of movement.

Auto Lock Stitch: Most digital (computerized) machines have this facility. At the touch of a button, a tiny knot is sewn at the start and end of the seam.

Auto Thread Trimmer: Feature that's generally found on middle range to high end machines. By touching a button, the thread tails are neatly trimmed and tied off at the end of sewing a seam.

Auto Tension: A term generally used to describe the machine's upper thread tension being trouble free. Ideally, the tension should only require altering for special effects such as gathering or to produce loose basting / tacking stitches, or where unusual threads are being used. For normal sewing, using a quality thread and correct needle type and size, a good machine will sew most delicate fabrics up to heavyweight without having to change the tension.

Awl: Pointed tipped tool for pushing out corners such as when fabric is turned right way.

SEWING TERMS BEGINNING WITH

B

Baby Pique Knit: A knitting method that creates a fine, small textured surface that appears similar to a very small waffle weave.

Back Appliqué: A piece of fabric used behind a design where the front fabric will be cut away to reveal the fabric beneath it (also known as Reverse Appliqué).

Backing: A quilting term for the back layer of fabric used in a quilt, wall hanging etc.

Backstitch: Either a hand stitch – that is formed by overlapping stitches, first stitch up to front of work, second, back behind first needle position and then up again in front, repeat along the row, OR reverse stitching on sewing machine, used at the beginning and end of a row of stitches to secure in place.

Back-Tack: Using the reverse stitch facility to make a few stitches to secure the seam at the beginning and end. All sewing machines have this feature. Most digital (computerized) machines can also perform this function automatically.

Back Yoke: A piece of fabric that connects the back of a garment to the shoulders. This allows the garment to lay flat and drape nicely.

Balance Wheel: The hand wheel that's located on the side of the machine. Rotating the wheel manually will move the needle up and down. Always rotate the wheel towards you when the machine is threaded, otherwise thread tangling will occur.

Ballpoint Needles: These needles have slightly

rounded tips and are designed to part the fibres of knit fabrics rather than piercing them to prevent damaging fabric.

Bar-Tack: To reinforce a seam with a bar of stitches, providing a more durable seam end. Commonly used at stress points.

Bar-Tack: Bar-tacks are found at the ends of a buttonhole. They are also used to attach belt loops to garments and for securing the corners of pockets and other parts of garments. Most machines can make bar-tacks by using a basic zigzag stitch. Some digital (computerized) machines have a special automatic bar-tack function.

Base Layer: Worn next to the skin, a base layer wicks sweat and keeps the wearer drier and more comfortable.

Basting Stitch: In sewing terms, basting is a type of tacking stitch that's used to temporarily hold the garment together allowing it to be tried on for fitting, prior to final sewing. The basting stitch should be quite loose, allowing easy removal. Some high end sewing machines feature an automatic basting stitch. However, basting can be achieved on almost all sewing machines by setting the stitch length to maximum and gradually reducing the upper thread tension until the stitches become suitably loose to allow easy removal.

Batten: This is a length of wood to attach a blind, pelmet or valance to a window frame.

Batting: American term for wadding

Basting: Large stitching to temporarily join a seam. It is removed when permanent stitching is done. Basting can either be done by hand or by machine. (Also known as tacking).

Beading Needle: Sharp, very fine needle with long thin shaft to go through beads; sizes 10 to 16.

Bed Valance: This a fabric skirt covering the bed divan (also known as Dust Skirt / Ruffles).

Bias: This is the most stretchable part of the fabric. The true bias is 45 degrees from straight of grain (selvedge) or put simply diagonally.

Bias Binding: Strips of fabric cut on the bias.

Bias Cut: A technique used by designers for

cutting clothing to utilize the greater stretch in the "bias" or diagonal direction of the fabric, thereby causing it to accentuate body lines and curves and drape softly.

Bias Tape: A strip cut from the bias of the fabric which can be used to neaten edges and fit around curves. Most bias tapes are double folded, with long edges turned to inside approximately 6 mm (1/4") and then folded in half.

Binding: Encasing of raw edges.

Bird Nesting: A name given to the threads caught between the fabric and the needle plate which resemble a bird's nest. This can be caused by problems with the upper thread tension such as upper thread not going through the take-up lever, upper thread not following the correct path, or improper hooping.

Bishop's Sleeve Curtains: This style of curtain is made longer and pulled up and draped over the tied section.

Blanket Stitch: Used to neaten edge of buttonholes and fabric edges, blanket stitch is formed by looping thread around needle so that a line of thread is on the edge. Can be done by machine or hand.

Blanket Stitch: A decorative stitch often used to finish an unhemmed blanket. The stitch can be seen on both sides of the blanket.

Blend: A yarn or a fabric that is made up of more than one type of fiber.

Blind: A single curtain with a fixed heading which pulls up from the bottom.

Blind Hem Foot: A specially designed presser foot for use with the above. Supplied as standard with many machines but may be an optional accessory with more basic models.

Blind Hem Stitch: Blind hemming (or invisible hemming) is normally found on the bottom of skirts, trousers and quality made curtains. The hem is sewn from the inside without the stitching showing through on the outside. Most sewing machines have this facility. It is also known as a 'Catch Stitch'.

Block: A quilting term referring to the individual unit used in a quilt top.

Bobbin: Spool or reel that holds the lower

thread in a sewing machine; this thread combines with top thread to form stitches on the fabric. The bobbin thread shows on the underside.

Bobbin Case: This is the unit holding the bobbin in place within the lower part of the sewing machine.

Bobbin Embroidery: Designs worked with the fabric positioned face down with the specialty thread wound onto the bobbin. Use for threads that are too heavy or thick for the needle.

Bobbin Tension: Term used to describe the tensioning of the bobbin thread. This is normally a factory setting but can be adjusted by the small adjusting screw on the bobbin case.

Bobbin Winder: Component part of the machine that winds thread onto the bobbin. On nearly all machines, the winder automatically stops when the bobbin is full. The sewing mechanism should be disengaged when bobbin winding; on most machines, this will happen when the winder is engaged.

Bobbling: Also known as Pilling: this is the term used to describe the tiny fabric balls that occur after repeated wear. They can be removed with a fabric shaver. The better the quality of fabric, the less it will bobble.

Bodice: The part of the garment that fits the torso (running from shoulder to waist).

Bolt: Fabric is stored on a roll known as a bolt, and is folded right sides together lengthwise on the bolt.

Bonding: The technique of permanently joining together two fabrics or layers of fabrics together by a bonding agent into one unit.

Bonded Fleece: Multiple layers of fleece are bonded together to form a higher functioning garment.

Boning: Thin nylon or plastic strips used to stiffen and shape close fitting garments such as bodices. If your first thought was something entirely different, then you should be thoroughly ashamed of yourself!

Border Print: Patterns which are printed along one edge, and a narrow strip down the side for hems. Sari fabric frequently has a border print and also often used for skirts, tablecloths and bedding.

Bound Edge: A technique using bias binding that neatens a raw edge.

Box Pleat: A single, uniform fold in the center back of a garment to allow for more room and comfort.

Box Pleats: A row of pleats that are folded in alternating directions.

Braid: A flat decorative trim.

Breathability: The movement of air from one side of the fabric to the other to keep the wearer comfortable. The breathability rating is typically expressed in a gram measurement of how much vapor a square meter (G/M2) of fabric will allow to pass in a 24-hour period (typically, 1,000G/M2 to 10,000000G/M2). Generally, the higher the number, the more breathable the garment.

Brushed: A finishing process for knit or woven fabrics in which brushes or other abrading devices are used to raise a nap on fabrics or create a novelty surface texture.

Bullion: A thick twisted decorative fringe.

Bust Line: The horizontal line running across the back and around the fullest part of the bust. It is important to get this measurement correct when sizing patterns.

Bust Point: The point on the pattern where the point of the bust should fall.

Button-Down Collar: Found on many men's dress wovens, where the collar's wings can be buttoned to the front of the shirt, minimizing the spread between the wings.

Buttonhole: A bound slit in the fabric to allow button to pass through for closure.

Buttonhole Stitch: Hand stitch used to neaten and strengthen the raw edges of buttonholes. Resembles satin stitch. Most modern machines stitch buttonholes automatically.

Buttonhole (1 Step) Auto Sizing:
Automatically produces a buttonhole to match the size of the button being used on the garment. The size is gauged by placing a button (from the garment) into a receptacle in the buttonhole presser foot. Buttonhole is then sewn out in one, non-stop operation and can easily be repeated throughout the garment. The main benefits with

this system are: very easy to use, perfectly neat, every buttonhole is the same size. Digital sewing machines feature several buttonhole styles, the main ones are: standard (used for blouses, dresses, skirts) keyhole (for jackets, coats, denims) and stretch (for garments made in jersey fabric).

Buttonhole (4 Step): This system is generally found on basic machines. The process is far more complicated than the 1-step system because the buttonhole is produced in four stages with the size of each buttonhole being individually marked out. Beginning with the buttonhole dial set at stage one: the first side of the buttonhole is sewn until the length is reached and sewing is then paused. The dial must then be set to stage two and a few bar-tack stitches are sewn and then paused. The dial is then turned to stage three and the second side of the buttonhole is sewn and then paused. Finally the dial is set to stage four to sew the second bar-tack.

Button Sew on Foot: Specially designed presser foot that allows you to use the machine to sew buttons onto a garment – great time saver if you have a lot of buttons to sew.

Button-Through Sleeve Placket: A small

placket located near the end of the sleeve, by the cuff, which contains a single button closure.

SEWING TERMS BEGINNING WITH

C

Cafe Curtains: A curtain which fits the bottom half of a window but let's in the light at the top. (Also known as Cottage Blinds).

CamoHex (Sport-Tek): A sublimated digital camouflage that uses small hexagons in a tonal pattern.

Capped Sleeve: This is a very short sleeve that does not extend below the under arm level.

Card: Disk which is inserted into a computerized embroidery machine onto which embroidery designs are or can be saved.

Carded Ring Spun Cotton: Carded yarns have not been combed. They contain a wider range of fiber lengths and, as a result, are not as uniform or as strong as combed yarns.

Cased Heading: This is a channel at the curtain top which enables you to thread a curtain rod through.

Casing: A fabric layer that encases either elastic or a drawstring.

Casing: A stitched channel between two pieces of fabric to hold either a length of dowelling or a curtain rod.

Casual Microfiber: Tightly woven fabric from a very fine polyester thread, usually with a sueded finish for a soft feel. Inherently water repellent and wind resistant due to its construction. 100% polyester microfiber.

Catch Stitch: Aka, Blind Hemming Stitch.

CB Bobbin (front load bobbin): The term given to machines where the bobbin is located at the front of the machine and accessed by opening a drop down cover.

CB Shuttle (Hook): Part of the sewing mechanism associated with the above. Connects the upper and lower threads to form the stitch.

Chambray: A plain woven fabric that can be made from silk or manufactured fibers, but is most commonly cotton. It incorporates a colored warp and white filling yarns.

Chenille Needle: Needle with a sharp point and a large eye, shorter than embroidery needles; sizes 18-24.

Chinese Collar: This is a short unfolded stand-up collar which starts at the neckline and stands vertically 2-3cm (also known as a Mandarin collar).

Chin Guard: A fold of soft fabric around the end of the zipper that helps prevent abrasion. Also known as a zipper garage.

Clapper: A wooden pressing aid, with different angled sides to help press tailored garments as they are sewn, providing crisp edges, points and curves.

Cleat: A two pronged hook which is fixed to one side of the window frame to secure the cords when a blind is pulled up.

Clean Finish: Term used to describe the way the raw edge is finished if not being stitched later: Stitch 6 mm (1/4?) from the edge and press to wrong side then stitch down.

Clip: Term used to trim the inside curve to allow seams to lie flat.

Clip-on Presser Foot (snap on presser feet): This term describes the way that the presser foot is attached to the machine. Most modern machines take clip on feet. However, it's very important when purchasing additional presser feet that they're suitable for your particular make and model. For example: a clip on foot for a Brother won't work on a Janome.

Coil (OGIO): A metallic colored coil zipper.

Collar: The upright or turned-over neckband of a coat, jacket or shirt.

Collar Stand: On a woven shirt, the collar stand is around the neck and placed between the actual collar and the shirt. This stand raises the collar so it's finished edge will fall smoothly back over the neck edge.

Colorfast: A dyed fabric's ability to resist fading due to washing, exposure to sunlight and other environmental conditions.

Combed Ring Spun Cotton: A process by which the short fibers of a yarn are removed and the remaining longer fibers are arranged in parallel order for a high- quality yarn with excellent strength, fineness and uniformity.

Combination Rods: This is where two or three curtain tracks share one set of brackets and used to give windows a layered look.

Computerized Embroidery Machines: These machines will only produce embroidery (as mentioned above) they can't be used for sewing.

Computerized Sewing Machines: In comparison to mechanical machines, computerized or digital sewing machines are designed and engineered for easy operation. Stitches are selected simply by touching a button.

Important stitch settings such as stitch length and width are automatically chosen for you, but can be varied if required. Whereas with a mechanical machine, you'll have a lot more to contend with whenever you want to change a stitch – i.e. lots of levers knobs and dials!

Computerized Sewing & Embroidery Machines: These are sewing machines like the computerized ones mentioned above but can also produce large, multi-colored embroidery and large lettering. Designs can be selected from the machine's built in library, downloaded from the web or created on your computer using digitizing embroidery software.

Concealed Zip Foot: Essential presser foot that's used for inserting concealed (invisible) zips into dresses, skirts, etc. When correctly fitted, the zip is completely hidden.

Contour: With curve. For instance pattern cutting can be cut on a curve which helps garments to fit better such as contour waistbands.

Cord Locks: A stopper or toggle on a drawcord that keeps the cord from retracting into the garment.

Cording: This is a twisted rope that is used in piping or as a drawstring. Cording can be covered with bias fabric strips to make piping.

Corduroy: A cut filling pile cloth with narrow to wide ribs. Usually made of cotton, but can be found in polyester and other synthetic blends.

Cornice: Another name for a Pelmet.

Cottage Blind: A curtain which fits the bottom half of a window but let's in the light at the top. (also known as Cafe Curtains).

Cotton: Soft vegetable fiber obtained from the seedpod of the cotton plant.

Cotton Count: A measure of thread density. It is the amount of thread measured in "hanks" (840 yards) needed to create one pound. With this system, the higher the number, the finer the yarn. In the United States, a cotton count between one and 20 is referred to as course counts. A regular single knit t-shirt can be between 15-18 count and a fashion tee is usually in the 30-40 count range.

Covered Buttons: A button covered with fabric; usually to match the garment.

Cover-Seamed: A finish in which two needles are used to create parallel rows of visible stitching. It is used around the neck, armholes, waistband and wrists of garments to create a cleaner, more durable finish.

Crewel Needles: Long sharp needle with large eyes; size 1-10.

Critically Seam-Sealed: Select (or critical) seams are taped with waterproof tape. This helps prevent moisture from getting in through the seams where it is most likely to occur—such as the shoulders, armholes or hood.

Cross Grain: Cut at right angles to the grain line, across the grain. Border prints are usually cut this way.

Cross Stitch: Two stitches that cross each other diagonally to form one stitch in the shape of a cross. Usually done by hand but nowadays some machines offer this as a stitch.

Crossways Fold: A width-ways fold of fabric which accommodates wider pattern pieces.

Cuff: The part of the sleeve encircling the wrist.

Also the turned-back hem of a trouser leg.

Curved Seam: A seam stitched by machine with two different shaped edges that when joined shapes the garment. Used at bust and waist and hip areas. Also known as a 'Princess Seam'.

Custom Designs: Designs which are created by digitizing artwork or manipulating existing patterns.

Cut Width: This is the width of fabric needed including seams or hems.

Cutting Line: Found on paper patterns. This is the outermost dark line which is marked with the size.

SEWING TERMS BEGINNING WITH

D

Darning Needle: Sharp sewing needle with small eye.

Dart: A tapered fold in a garment/pattern to allow for fullness usually in the bust, waist and back areas which helps to shape garment to body contours.

Deboss. To depress below the surrounding fabric surface for decoration or lettering. Often confused with embossing which is to raise in relief from a surface.

DC Motor: This type of motor can now be found on many sewing machines. The main benefit is a more easily managed sewing speed that can be varied from incredibly slow to fast. At slow speed however, there's no loss of force behind the needle. This allows you to sew slowly over thick seams or heavyweight fabric without stalling.

Decorative Stitches: Small stitch patterns that are used to decorate garments, craft projects, table linens, soft furnishings, etc. Not normally found on basic machines, but are a feature on middle range models upwards. The choice varies depending on make and model of machine.

Denier: A system of measuring the weight of a continuous filament fiber. The lower the number, the finer the fiber; the higher the number, the heavier the fiber.

Density: This is the number of stitches used in a particular area.

Digitizing: The changing of artwork which can be read by a computerized embroidery sewing machine via a card (disk).

Directional Stitching: 1 All sewing lines follow the direction of the fabric grain – also known as 'stroking the cat' (to find the direction of the grain, run finger along cut edge and stitch in direction in which fibres curl smoothly). 2. In dressmaking, directional stitching refers to stitching every seam in the same direction, ie: all seams waist to hem in order to prevent seams puckering or stretching. 3. On a sewing machine, this refers to multi-directional stitching including side to side (not just forwards and backwards).

District Fit: District has a slim fit that is close to the body. The styles have shorter sleeves and tighter and higher armholes than District Made.

District Made Fit: District Made has a comfortable fit with a relaxed waist. The styles have a longer sleeve and relaxed and lower armholes than District.

Dolman Sleeve: This type of sleeve is an extension of the bodice and can be loose or close fitting (also known as Kimono sleeve) – although we would say that dolman sleeves tend to be longer in length and closer fitting whilst Kimono sleeves tend to have a wide square look with a looser fitting.

Dongle: A security device, which attaches to the printer, between embroidery machine and computer to prevent unlicensed file sharing or misuse.

Double Hem: Folding the fabric over twice in equal amounts.

Dowelling: A circular length of wood/plastic attached to the back of a blind to keep the fabric flat.

Dust Skirt/Ruffles: A fabric skirt covering the bed divan. (also known as Bed valance).

Dobby: A decorative weave, usually geometric, that is woven into the fabric. Standard dobby fabrics are usually flat and relatively fine or sheer.

Dolman Sleeve: A sleeve tapered from a very large armhole to fit closely at the wrist. Usually cut in one piece with the body of the garment.

Double Knit: A circular knit fabric knitted via double stitch on a double needle frame to provide a double thickness.

Double-Needle Stitching: A finish commonly used on a sleeve or bottom hem that uses two needles to create parallel rows of visible stitching, giving the garment a cleaner, more finished look, as well as adding durability.

Down: The soft, fluffy under feathers of ducks and geese. Serves as an excellent outerwear thermal insulator.

Dri-FIT (NIKE GOLF): Fabric that helps keep the wearer comfortable and dry by moving perspiration from the skin, through the layers of fabric, to the outside layer for rapid evaporation across the outer surface area.

Dri-Mesh® Polyester: The double layer mesh construction releases heat and sweat, while maintaining breathability. 100% polyester double mesh.

Drop Feed: Allows the machines teeth (feed dogs) to be lowered for free motion sewing. It's also used for machine darning and lets you use the machine to sew on buttons when used with the special presser foot.

Drop-in Bobbin (top load bobbin): This was introduced for easier bobbin insertion. The bobbin just drops into the bed of the machine where it's more accessible; as opposed to having a separate bobbin case (CB bobbin) which can be a bit of a fiddle. Most modern machines that use this system won't require oiling. In addition, the system is less prone to thread jamming. The plate that covers the bobbin is usually transparent allowing you to check on the available amount of bobbin thread prior to sewing.

Drop Needle: A knit fabric characterized by vertical lines within the cloth. Manufactured by dropping a needle from the knitting cylinder.

Drop Tail: A longer back than front for the purpose of keeping the shirt tucked in. Also referred to as Extended Tail.

Dry Zone® Technology: A double-layer polyester fabrication that wicks moisture away from the body.

Dyed-To-Match: A term which characterizes buttons or trims that are the same color as the garment onto which they are sewn.

Dual Feed (even feed, walking foot): Prevents fabric layers from creeping or shifting. Usually this is an additional presser foot that works in place of the standard foot. Slippery fabrics such as satin will pucker the seam when sewn using the standard foot. This happens because the lower layer of fabric feeds through a little more quickly than upper layer. It is a big problem when sewing quilt layers or when keeping striped or patterned fabrics matched up whilst being sewn. The dual feed has its own built in feed teeth which work in unison with the teeth on the machine, so that both fabric layers are fed along equally. Some high end machines have built in dual feed.

Duck Cloth: Tightly woven, plain-weave, bottom-weight fabric with a hard, durable finish that provides wind and snag resistance.

Durable Water Repellent: A DWR treatment involves applying a coating to a jacket's outermost fibers to prevent precipitation from saturating the jacket's exterior.

SEWING TERMS BEGINNING WITH

E

Ease: The amount of excess provided for ease of movement in a garment. There is often wearing ease and designer ease. Wearing ease is calculated to allow garments to move with the body etc. Designer ease is the style element and varies according to the designer's wishes.

Ease Stitch: This is simply a row of slightly longer than usual stitches just within seam allowance, used to make a larger or curved piece of fabric fit on to another by evenly pulling in the extra fabric without making any gathers or tucks in the larger piece of fabric.

Edge Stitching: A row of stitching on the edge of a garment, usually 3 mm (1/8") from edge.

Emblem: Embroidered design with a neatened (usually overlocked or hot cut) edge which can be used on a garment for decoration.

Embroidery: Decorative stitches used to create a pattern on fabric.

Embellish: The addition of decorative stitching, appliqué and trims to a sewing project or garment.

Entredeux: A French word for 'something placed between two things'. This is a lacy trim or stitch that has heavily embroidered holes. The Entredeux tape is used in between two fabric pieces to provide a decorative joining piece. Entredeux stitch can be made using a wing needle which leaves holes as it stitches.

Envelope Curtains: These curtains are static and don't pull back and the bottom inside corners are pinned back to let light in.

Enzyme Washed: A laundering process in which a catalytic substance is added to create a chemical change in the fabric resulting in a very soft finish, smoother appearing surface and reduced shrinkage.

Epaulet (Epaulette): An ornamental fabric strip or loop sewn across the shoulder of a shirt, dress or coat.

Ergonomic: Design elements incorporated into a garment to improve the design by enhancing the wearer's comfort, performance or health.

Etched Tone Buttons: A more upscale horn tone button with an etched pattern.

Even Feed: Aka, Dual Feed.

Extended Tail: A longer back than front for the purpose of keeping the shirt tucked in. Also referred to as Drop Tail.

Eyelets: Small holes or perforations made in a series to allow for breathability. Finished with either stitching or brass grommets.

Extension Table: Large, slide-on table that

greatly increases the size of the sewing bed. Usually an optional extra, but supplied as standard on some machines.

SEWING TERMS BEGINNING WITH

F

Fabric Diagonals: A fabric that is printed on a diagonal. Check that a fabric has this if you want to match diagonal prints.

Face: The outside or 'right' side of a fabric, the side you see when the garment is finished.

Facing: A garment section that is turned to the inside to hide raw edges of seams without hems, such as necklines, front edges, armholes.

Fat Quarter: Originally a quilting term but also used for wearable art. Fat Quarters are cut differently and measure a 'squared' ¼ yard of fabric (18 x 22") rather than the usual long cut across the width ¼ yard (approx 9 x 45").

Feather Stitch: A machine stitch used to join non-fraying pieces of fabrics to each other.

Feed Dogs: These are the jagged teeth under the throat plate on a sewing machine that go up and down to push the fabric along whilst sewing.

Festoon Blind: Festoon blind is ruched from top to bottom.

Fill-Power: The measure of the loft or "fluffiness" of a down garment that is loosely related to the insulating value of the down. The higher the fill power, the more trapped air an ounce of the down can trap, and thus the more insulating ability an ounce of the down will have.

Fill Stitch: A group of running stitches which are used to cover an area of fabric.

Finger Pressing: Used on small areas of fabric, simply use your fingers to flatten the seams open.

Finial: A decorative end for a curtain pole.

Finished Width: The actual width after the treatment is finished and all allowances have been used.

Finishing: The term used to finish off the edge of garments, such as neatening seam allowances, removing excess stabilizers etc.

Fix Stitch: The small stitches on the spot that are done at the start and end of a seam to stop it unraveling (also known as 'Lock stitch').

Flagging: This happens to fabric that has been hooped incorrectly which causes an up and down motion resulting in thread bird-nesting and does not allow stitches to form correctly.

Flame-Resistant: These fabrics and garments are intended to resist ignition, prevent the spread of flames away from the immediate area of high heat impingement and to self-extinguish almost immediately upon removal of an ignition source. FR clothing is NOT fireproof.

Flat Back Mesh: A double-ply polyester knit fabric consisting of an open-hole mesh layer with a polyester layer behind to make it "flat back".

You get the breathability of mesh without showing any skin.

Flat Collar/Cuffs: A single ply fabric with a finished edge that is used for collars and cuffs on sport shirts and short sleeve garments. Also known as welt.

Flat Felled Seam: A very durable seam created by sewing the wrong sides of the fabric together and then trimming one of the seams and turning the other seam allowance under and stitching over the trimmed seam. Good for jeans and reinforced seams.

Flatlock Stitching: Made by bringing two raw fabric edges together and covering them with machine stitching.

Float: Long satin stitches that lay on the top of a design.

Fold Line: This indicates that a paper pattern piece needs to be placed on the fold of the fabric so that two identical halves are cut as one thus avoiding center seams.

Foot Control (foot pedal): Supplied with all sewing machines. Works in the same way as your car's accelerator pedal: the further down you press - the faster you go!

Foot Pressure: This is the amount of weight that the presser foot applies to the fabric as the stitch is being formed. On many machines this can be varied to accommodate different types of fabric.

Frame: The holding device for an embroidery hoop.

Freehand Foot: Used for free-motion work. Makes it easier to move the fabric, provides better visibility, prevents stitches from skipping and snagging (Also referred to as Darning Foot, Quilting Foot, Embroidery Foot).

Free-Arm (sleeve-arm): This facility is found on almost all sewing machines. Part of the machine's work surface can be removed, allowing the sewing bed to convert to a narrower shape. This allows sleeves, trouser bottoms and awkward shapes to be positioned over and around the free-arm to enable easier access for sewing.

Free Motion: Embroidery that is done free hand by lowering the feed dogs on the sewing machine, so that the work can be moved in any direction at any speed. Usually worked with the fabric in a hoop and using a darning or embroidery foot. Stitch length is determined by how quickly the work is moved, quickly for long stitches, slowly for small stitches.

French Curve: A tool used for creating curves for pattern design.

French Seam: This is a seam finish that encloses the raw edges so that the reverse side is neat. To create, stitch a 1 cm (3/8") seam with WRONG sides together. Trim to 3 mm (1/8"), turn through and press with seam on fold and RIGHT sides together. Stitch again taking 6 mm (1/4") seam. Press again. an enclosed seam which is very narrow and ideal for sheer fabrics where seams are on show.

Frill: A longer length of fabric gathered or pleated onto an edge for decoration.

Frog Fastening: A narrow fabric tube which forms a loop to fasten with a round button. Also known as a 'Rouleau Loop'.

Front Load Bobbin: Exactly the same as CB Bobbin.

Fullness Ratio: This is the ratio of fabric width to the width of the window. Curtains are usually at least twice the window width.

Fusible: The term used to describe a fine mist of adhesive on fabric or interfacings that when pressed with hot iron, sticks them to another fabric.

French Cuff: A shirt cuff that is folded back before fastening, creating a double- layered cuff.

French Terry Cotton: The knit jersey version of terry cloth. It features loops of pile on one side and a smooth, brushed finish on the other for softness and a lived-in, vintage look.

Full Cut: Refers to a garment's fit as being generous and roomy.

Fully Fashioned: A garment that's knitted to fit the shape of the body.

Fully Seam-Sealed: Every seam throughout the jacket is sealed with waterproof tape to help prevent water from leaking in.

SEWING TERMS BEGINNING WITH

G

Garment Dyed: A dyeing process that occurs after the garment is assembled.

Garment Washed: A wash process where softeners are added to finished garments to help the cotton fibers relax. The result is a fabric with a thicker appearance, reduced shrinkage and a softer hand.

Gather: A technique for gathering longer lengths of fabric into a smaller length. Used to create fullness or allow several pieces of fabric of different lengths to fit together. This is done by stitching one or two rows of long basting stitch and leaving long threads at either end. If working on a sewing machine, pull up bobbin thread.

Gathering (by machine): Most machines are capable of producing gathers in lightweight woven fabrics. There are several techniques, but the most common method is to set the stitch length to maximum and gradually increase the upper tension until the desired effect is achieved. You can also try sewing with a loose upper tension, then after fastening the threads at one end you can draw up the lower thread to gather the fabric as required.

Gathering Foot: Specially designed presser foot for gathering. Some versions have a slot that will allow you to gather one layer of fabric whilst simultaneously stitching it onto a flat layer.

Godets: Usually triangularly shaped fabric inserts added to increase the swing and fullness of a skirt or dress.

Grain Line: This is the direction in which the threads are woven. The straight grain runs parallel to the fabric selvedge. Crosswise grain runs at right angles to the selvedge (across the width).

Grade Seam: This eliminates bulk from the seams; trim the outer seam allowances to 6 mm (1/4") and the under seam allowance to a scant 3 mm (1/8").

Grosgrain: A firm, closely woven fabric with narrow horizontal stripes. Commonly used for ribbons, neckties and trimmings.

Guide Stitch: Stitches used to align embroideries when using several hoops or that assist in fabric placement for appliqué.

Gusset: A piece of fabric sewn into the seamline to provide fullness.

SEWING TERMS BEGINNING WITH

H

Header: The extra fabric above a cased heading which forms a frill.

Heading Tape: A wide woven tape that has slots for curtains hooks and includes the gathering cords.

Hem: The fabric which is turned up on the edge of the garment to provide a neat finished edge.

Hem Allowance: Amount of fabric allowed for the hemming.

Herringbone: A chevron or zig-zag pattern knit into fabric. Commonly used in golf shirts and twill shirts.

High Bust: This is the measurement taken above the full bust measurement under the arms and around the back and chest. If this measurement is more than 5 cm (2") larger than the full bust measurement then dress, jacket and top pattern size should be selected by the high bust size and alterations made to fit the fuller cup.

High Profile: A term used for a cap or hat silhouette that is less fitted to the head with a high slope. Usually structured with buckram or other stiff fabric lining.

Hip Point: The point on the pattern where the hip comes.

Hong Kong Seam: A seam finishing method of binding the seam allowance to encase raw edges. On lightweight fabrics, both seam allowances can be pressed to one side and then bound together. On medium and heavier weight fabrics, press seam open and bind each seam allowance separately.

Hook and Eye: A two-part closure that consists of a hook and an eye.

Hook and Loop: A fastener closure system. The rough side is called the hook. Its softer mate is called loop. The hooks engage into the loop and provide the closure. More commonly known as VELCRO®.

Hoop: Made up of two rings, one slightly smaller than the other, that fit together to clamp fabric tightly in place.

Horn Tone Buttons: Buttons that appear to be manufactured from horn.

Houndstooth: A medium-sized broken check effect that is knit into the fabric.

SEWING TERMS BEGINNING WITH

I

In-Seam: The inside leg seam that runs from crotch to hem.

Interfacing: A fine fabric used between layers of fabric in a garment to provide stability and shape. Used in cuffs, collars, plackets, waistbands.

Interlining: Another fabric layer, usually cut and sewn as one with main fabric, to provide support to main fabric. Also known as Underlining.

Inverted Pleat: A flat pleat with the extra fabric to the wrong side.

Insulated Jacket: A jacket designed to hold body heat close and buffer surrounding cold air. Down, fleece and synthetic fibers are common insulators. Insulation levels help determine warmth ratings.

Interlock Knit: A two-ply fabric knit simultaneously to form one thicker and heavier ply. It has more natural stretch than a jersey knit, a soft hand, and the same appearance and feel on both sides. Commonly used in knit shirts and turtlenecks.

SEWING TERMS BEGINNING WITH
J

Jacquard Knit: Often an intricate pattern knit directly into the fabric during the manufacturing process. Typically, two or more colors are used.

Jersey Knit: The consistent interloping of yarns in the jersey stitch to produce a fabric with a smooth, flat face and a more textured, but uniform back.

SEWING TERMS BEGINNING WITH

K

Kangaroo Pocket: Another name for a front pouch pocket in a sweatshirt or t-shirt. Called a split kangaroo pocket in a full-zip garment.

Kick Pleats: Similar to box pleats but folds are further apart and don't butt together at the back.

Kimono: Term used to describe a traditional Japanese dress. The basic kimono is a square-cut body with square-cut sleeves and has remained much the same since the 10th century.

Kimono Sleeve: This type of sleeve is an extension of the bodice and can be loose or close fitting (also known as Dolman sleeve) – although we would say that dolman sleeves tend to be longer in length and closer fitting whilst Kimono sleeves tend to have a wide square look with a looser fitting.

Knee Lifter (knee operated presser foot):
Found on some higher end machines but originally developed for industrial machines. The knee lifter is a specially designed metal rod that pushes into the front of the machine. The rod is shaped so that it bends down to rest against your knee. Moving your knee onto the rod will lift or lower the presser foot. This may at first sound like a rather weird set up, but it will keep both hands free to manipulate the fabric – ideal when you've several small pieces of fabric to line up under the foot. The knee lifter is easily pulled out from the machine when not required.

Knife Pleats: A row of folds all in the same direction.

SEWING TERMS BEGINNING WITH
L

Lambrequin: A pelmet which extends down the side of the window.

Lap Shoulders (Rabbit Skins): A detail in infant tees and bodysuits in which the fabric overlaps at the neckline and shoulders for easier changing.

LCD Screen: Found on digital (computerised) machines. The screen displays your chosen stitch and various settings such as stitch length and width. It will also advise on which presser foot to use for the given task.

Linen: A fabric made from linen fibers obtained from inside the woody stem of the flax plant. Linen fibers are much stronger and more lustrous than cotton. Linen fabrics are very cool and absorbent, but wrinkle easily, unless blended with manufactured fibers.

Lining: Used to finish the inside of a garment to hide seam construction, prevents 'see-through' and help garment to hang better.

Locker Loop: A looped piece of fabric in the neck of a garment for the convenience of hanging the garment on a hook. Can also be located at the center of the back yoke on the inside or outside of a garment.

Locker Patch: A semi-oval panel sewn into the inside back portion of a garment, just under the collar seam to reinforce the garment and minimize stretching when hung on a hook. The patch also allows for the garment tag or label to be sewn below the neckline to help prevent irritation.

Lock Stitch: The small stitches on the spot that are done at the start and end of an embroidery or seam to stop it unravelling. Also known as 'Fix stitch' and 'Loop stitch'.

Loom State: Refers to fabric that is straight from the loom that has overgone any finishing or dying processes. Loom state cloth will shrink, and needs to be prewashed before using.

Loop Stitch: Aka Lock Stitch.

Low Impact Technology (L.I.T.): Enhances the softness and performance of 100% polyester fleece in that the yarns are able to accept dye more readily which uses less water and energy than standard dyeing procedures.

Low Profile: A term used for a cap or hat silhouette that is more closely fitted to the head. Can be either structured or unstructured.

SEWING TERMS BEGINNING WITH

M

Machine Embroidery: Decorative stitching created by using decorative stitches on a sewing machine such as satin stitch and zigzag. Mid to top range machines have a number of embroidery stitches built-in. Also term used to denote embroidery pictures and motifs.

Machine Tacking: This is a loose tension stitch done by machine used to temporarily hold fabric in position before stitching permanently.

Mandarin Collar: This is a short unfolded stand-up collar which starts at the neckline and stands vertically 2-3 cms (also known as a Chinese collar).

Marking: Temporary marks made on fabric to aid positioning of pockets, buttonholes etc and on embroidery, used to determine how to hoop fabric.

Matte Taslan: A durable and water repellent nylon fabric, used mainly in outerwear garments. Same properties and hand as traditional Taslan, but with a dull, matte finish.

Melange: A mix of different colors of yarns knit together to create a heathered effect.

Metafil: A needle with an elongated eye for use with metallic decorative threads.

Microburn®: 75/25 poly/ring spun cotton tees that have a rare blend of shades for an unusually lightweight feel and a one-of-a-kind look.

Microfiber: Tightly woven fabric from a very fine polyester thread, usually with a sueded finish for a soft feel. Inherently water repellent and wind resistant due to its construction.

Microfleece: Crafted from ultra-fine yarn, this lightweight, high-density fleece is brushed less than a regular fleece garment for softness and warmth without bulk.

Mid-Layer: Worn over the base layer, this layer traps warm air, breathes and helps maintain body heat.

Mid Profile: A term used for a cap or hat silhouette that is in between that of a High Profile and Low Profile. Most often structured with buckram.

Milliners Needle: Needle with a long shaft of equal diameter throughout the length.

Mitre: A method of neatly folding fabric or trim at corners.

Mitring: A way of folding the excess seam allowance to achieve a less bulky, sharp corner.

Mitten Cuffs: Cuffs that fold over (like mittens)

to completely cover the hands for additional warmth.

Modal Blend: A super soft fabric made of a blend of ring spun cotton/modal. Modal is soft, smooth and breathable with a texture similar to cotton or silk. It washes well and resists pilling, so the garment looks better, longer.

Modern Stretch Cotton: A breathable fabric made from a blend of cotton and spandex to provide a flattering stretch. 96% cotton. 4% spandex.

Monogram: Letters, usually initials, embroidered for decoration.

Mounted Sleeve: This type of sleeve is set into the armhole with a seam on the shoulder end (also known as a set-in sleeve).

SEWING TERMS BEGINNING WITH
N

Nailhead: A jacquard knitting pattern in which the jacquard forms a design similar to small nail heads.

Nap: A fuzzy, fur-like feel created when fiber ends extend from the basic fabric structure to the fabric surface. The fabric can be napped on one or both sides.

Narrow Hemmer Foot: Specially designed presser foot that produces narrow hems (usually 2mm/3mm) on lightweight woven fabrics. Ideally suitable for scarves, table napkins, handkerchiefs, etc.

Neckband: A strip of fabric sewn around the inside of the neck in a woven shirt.

Needle Plate: Metal plate (sometimes called throat plate) that's located below the presser foot.

Needle Position: The position of needle in relation to the presser foot. On many machines, this can be varied from left, centre, right. The right position makes it easier to sew piping, as well as making it easier to sew closer to edge of the fabric. The center position is most commonly used for regular sewing. Selecting the left position can help in eliminating problems encountered with delicate fabrics.

Needle Stop – Up/Down:
NEEDLE UP: Machine will stop sewing with the needle always in its uppermost position ready to remove the work. This is also the best position for avoiding errors when threading.

NEEDLE DOWN: Machine will stop sewing with the needle always in its lowest position so that the work can be pivoted. Cuts out the fuss when working on small pieces of fabric that require lots of corners to be sewn.

Needle Threader: Built in feature found on many sewing machines. It will eliminate the frustration from what should normally be a very simple task.

Network: The method of linking computer to digitiser to embroidery machine using a modem.

Non-Iron: A term characterizing fabric that has been chemically treated to resist wrinkles, eliminating the need for ironing.

Notch: Triangular or diamond shaped marks on the cutting lines of paper patterns used to match seams together at sides, back and front etc. 2. Triangular shapes cut OUT of outer curved seam allowances so that when turned through the fabric will lie flat.

Notions: The American term used to describe haberdashery; frequently used on paper patterns.

Notch Lapel: The most common lapel found on blazers. The "notch" is the opening where the bottom of the collar meets the top of the lapel at a 75–90 degree angle.

Nublend® Fleece: A combined knitting and

spinning process developed by JERZEES for the prevention of pilling.

Nylon: A synthetic fiber with high strength and abrasion resistance, low absorbency and good elasticity.

SEWING TERMS BEGINNING WITH

Open-End Cotton: Open end spinning is a technology to make yarns without a spindle. OE yarns have less twist but a more uniform, abrasion-resistant surface and are produced at much faster speeds than other spinning technologies. Fabrics made from OE yarns generally have a cleaner appearance, but are less soft than garments made with ring spun yarns.

Ottoman: A tightly woven, horizontal raised rib

textured knit.

Outer Layer: Worn over the base and mid-layers, this layer resists water and wind and has comfortable stretch for mobility.

Overdyed: A process in which yarn-dyed fabrics or piece-dyed garments are put through an additional dye color to create unique colors.

Overlock: An overcast stitch which encases the edge and helps neaten raw edges. Also known as 'serging.'

Overlocker: A purpose-made sewing machine that overlocks fabric, cutting the edge and sewing in the same pass. Can be 3-8 thread and be used for a variety of creative stitching although most well-known for seam neatening. Also known as Sergers.

Overlock Foot: Used with the machine's overlock stitch, it has a guide which helps keep the stitching in line along the fabric edge. In addition, It will prevent the fabric edge from curling.

Overlock Stitch: Used for neatening the frayed edge of fabric. Can be used to simultaneously sew and neaten two or more fabric layers. Better results are achieved when using an overlock foot. The end result is reasonably adequate in comparison to the superior results achieved on an overlocking machine.

SEWING TERMS BEGINNING WITH

P

Patch Pocket: A pocket attached to the outside of a garment.

Pattern: The template need to create an item. Commercial patterns provide tissue pieces.

Pattern Layout: Diagram found on commercial pattern instruction sheets which indicate how to lay out pattern pieces on the fabric.

Pattern Match: This describes the technique of matching patterns on right and left edges, for drapes etc and is used when working with specifically patterned fabric, checks or plaids. Cut each piece on a single layer of fabric. Lay cut piece next to remaining fabric so that next section can be placed with pattern matching at key points (bust, hip etc). Remember when cutting two of same pattern piece, the second one should be placed face down on the fabric to ensure a left and right.

Peached: A soft hand usually obtained by brushing or sanding the fabric lightly. Can be achieved with chemical or laundry abrasion to give the surface a velvet-like appearance and softness.

Peak Lapel: Traditionally the most formal of blazer lapels, it's defined by edges pointing upwards to the wearer's shoulders.

Pearlized Buttons: Buttons that have a pearl-colored hue.

Pelmet: A decorative way of concealing curtain tops and tracks. This is usually a flat panel which can be painted or covered with fabric.

Pelmet Board: A horizontal wooden shelf from which a pelmet or valance is hung.

Peter Pan Collar: This is a small, flat round cornered collar without a stand. Popular for women's and children's garments.

Peplum: A flared 'skirt' attached to jacket or top at waist creating a fuller style at hem.

Perfect Blend®: A 50/50 blend of ring spun combed cotton and poly which makes Perfect Blend tees as good or better than the finest purebred.

Perfect Tri®: 50/25/25 poly/ring spun combed cotton/rayon. The undeniably perfect combination of exceptional softness and laid-back style.

Perfect Weight® Cotton: This extra-fine gauge 32 singles 100% ring spun combed cotton yarn is known for its lightweight softness. It's then compacted to 4.3 ounces for long-term durability and shrink resistance. The result is garments that look and feel perfect wear after wear.

Petersham: A heavy duty waist banding, usually black and reinforced with a line of stitching to prevent it folding or rolling when worn.

Pewter Buttons: Buttons that have a dull, metallic hue.

Pewter and Horn Tone Buttons: Buttons that incorporate pewter and horn tone. Usually one encompasses the other.

Pick Stitch: This is a decorative hand stitch used on collars, cuffs, front facings etc. An alternative to top stitching.

Pile: Surface texture to fabric. Only some fabrics, like velvet, have a visible pile; when brushed it will look a different colour. When cutting out, ensure all pattern pieces are laid in the same direction on the fabric so that the pile is going in its natural direction. (Also known as Nap).

Pilling: also known as bobbling, this is the term used to describe the tiny fabric balls that occur after repeated wear. They can be removed with a fabric shaver. The better the quality of fabric, the less it will pill.

Pintuck: Raised narrowly sewn tucks in fabric that add decorative detail.

Picot: A series of small embroidered loops forming an ornamental edging on some ribbon and lace.

Piece Dyed: A dyeing process that occurs when the fabric is in yardage form after it has been knitted or woven, but before the garment is assembled.

Pigment-Dyed: A type of dye process used to create a distressed or washed look that results in soft, muted tones and a soft hand.

Pilling: A tangled ball of fibers that appears on the surface of a fabric as a result of wear or continued friction or rubbing on the surface of the fabric.

Pima Cotton: A term applied to extra-long staple cotton grown in the U.S., Peru, Israel and Australia. It can only be grown in select areas where the cotton is fully irrigated and benefits from a longer growing season for a softer, stronger cotton than standard cotton.

Pit Zips: Zippers placed in the armpits of a jacket to be used for quick ventilation.

Pique Knit: A knitting method that creates a fine

textured surface that appears similar to a waffle weave. Commonly used for polo shirts.

Placket: The part of the shirt or jacket where the garment fastens or buttons together. Types of plackets include: reverse (generally a ladies styles in which the buttons are on the opposite side of a men's garment), open (in which there are no buttons or fasteners) and decorative (non-functioning).

Pleat: A flat usually narrow fold made in a piece of cloth by pressing or sewing two parts of the cloth together.

Ply: Two or more yarns that have been twisted together.

Polyester: A strong, durable synthetic fabric with high strength and excellent resiliency. Low moisture absorbency allows the fabric to dry quickly.

Poly-Filled: A warm polyester lining found in the body or sleeves of outerwear.

Polypropylene: A very light, highly resistant, thermoplastic resin used to make coatings, packaging and fabrics.

Polyurethane Coating (PU Coating): A finish commonly used in winter jackets, rainwear and wind-wear to offer high performance water resistance, while maintaining the garment's breathability.

Ponte Knit: Ponte knits have the forgiveness of a knit, but the versatility of a woven. They're very stable with a nominal amount of stretching capability.

Popcorn Pique: Alternating rows of baby pique knit and a larger pique knit that resembles small circles knit closely together.

Poplin: A tightly woven, durable, medium-weight cotton or cotton blend made by using a rib variation of the plain weave which creates a slight ridge effect.

Port Pocket® Access: A zipper entry pocket that allows the garment to be hooped and embroidered without impacting the inside lining of the garment.

Pre-Shrunk: Fabrics or garments that have received a pre-shrinking treatment. Princess Seams. Short, stitched folds that taper to a point, typically used to shape women's garments.

Presser Foot: Holds the fabric in place as the stitch is being formed.

Presser Foot Lever: Lever located at rear of the machine that raises or lowers the presser foot.

Presser Foot Dial: See foot pressure.

PVC: A polyurethane coating that is added to make garments water resistant.

SEWING TERMS BEGINNING WITH

Q

Quilting: A fabric construction in which a layer of down or fiberfill is placed between two layers of fabric, and then held in place by stitching or sealing in a consistent, all-over pattern.

Quilting needle: Sharp short needle with a small eye; size 5-12, sometimes known as betweens.

SEWING TERMS BEGINNING WITH

R

Raglan sleeve: This type of sleeve is attached to the garment by a seam that runs diagonally down the front neckline to the underarm and up to the back of the neckline.

Rapid Dry Technology: Designed with a unique weave to wick away moisture from the body.

Raw edge: The edge of the fabric that has not

been stitched or finished.

Rayon: A manufactured fiber composed of regenerated cellulose, derived from wood pulp, cotton linters or other vegetable matter, with a soft hand. Frequently used for shirts and pants.

Reinforce: A term used to describe stitching over an area again to strengthen the seam. Used in areas of most stress such as crotch.

Resizing: the ability to change the scale of a design or pattern to fit.

Revere Collar: flat V-shaped collar often found on blouses.

Reverse Appliqué: A piece of fabric used behind a design where the front fabric will be cut away to reveal the fabric beneath it. (also known as Back Appliqué).

Reverse Coil Zipper: Unlike the basic coil zipper, a reverse coil zipper doesn't show its teeth from the front.

Reverse Placket: When the buttons on a placket are on the opposite side from a men's garment. Commonly done on women's styles.

Reverse Sewing: See Back-tack.

Rib Knit: A textured knit that has the appearance of vertical lines. It is highly elastic and retains its shape. Commonly used for sleeve and neck bands.

Right Side: The side of fabric that you wish to use as the outside; the side with printing or design. For some fabrics, such as linen, silk or polyester, it is difficult to distinguish the right or wrong side, in which case it doesn't matter.Revere collar: flat V-shaped collar often found on blouses.

Ring Spun: Yarn made by continuously twisting and thinning a rope of cotton fibers. The twisting makes the short hairs of cotton stand out, resulting in a stronger yarn with a significantly softer hand.

Rip-Stop Nylon: A lightweight, wind and water resistant plain weave fabric with large rib yarns that stop tears without adding excess weight. Often used in activewear.

Rise: This is the distance from hip to waist. Rise measurement is taken from the waist down to the upper leg side.

Rotary Hook: Part of the sewing mechanism. Connects the upper and lower threads to form the stitch. Machines with a drop-in bobbin have a rotary hook. They are less prone to thread jamming and run more smoothly than machines with a CB Shuttle Hook.

R-Tek® Fleece: An exclusive lightweight microfleece with a soft, plush hand and an anti-pill finish to resist pilling. 100% polyester.

Ruched: A gathered ruffle or pleat of fabric used for trimming or decorating garments.

Ruching: A French term which means to gather, ruffle or pleat the fabric.

Running Stitch: A stitch that is spaced equally, with the underside stitching being half the length of the external side.

SEWING TERMS BEGINNING WITH
S

Sand-washed: A process in which the fabric is washed with very fine lava rocks or rubber/silicon balls, resulting in a softer fabric with a relaxed look and reduced shrinkage.

Satin Jersey: This fabric has the drape and stretch of jersey plus a luxurious satin wash that sets it apart from other soft cotton and makes it noticeably smooth and sleek.

Satin Stitch: Zigzag where the stitches are formed very close together (no gaps between the zigs and the zags). Satin stitch has many uses, and is a particular favorite for sewing applique designs.

Satin Stitch Foot: Used in connection with the above. Designed to give better visibility and produce neater, more uniform stitching.

Scoop Neck: Characterized by a deep, rounded neckline that is significantly deeper than normal necklines. Typically found on women's shirts.

Sculpted Hem: A hem that is softly rounded for fashion detail and un-tucked wear.

Seam Allowance: The piece of fabric between the fabric edge and the stitching. This is usually 15 mm (5/8") for dressmaking. And 6 mm (1/4") for crafts.

Seam Line: The line on which to sew when putting a garment together and it is this seam line that must be matched when putting the garment together and not the raw edges.

Seam Ripper: A cutting tool used to undo seam stitching. Also known as 'A quick unpick'.

Seam Sealing: The process of treating the stitch holes and seams of a garment to prevent leaking and to ensure full waterproof integrity.

Self-Fabric Collar: A collar that is constructed from the same material as the body of the garment.

Self-Fabric Sweatband: Refers to a panel of fabric at the front of a cap that is constructed from the same fabric as the crown of the cap.

Selvedge: This is the bound side edges of the fabric which doesn't fray. (Also known as Selvage)

Separating Zip: A zipper that comes apart in two separate parts so the garment can open completely. Used on jackets and sportswear. (Also known as Open-ended zip.)

Serging: An overcasting technique done on the cut edge of the fabric to prevent unraveling.

Set-In Sleeve: Most common style of sleeve, which is sewn into the shoulder seam. Sherpa Fleece. A knit terry fabric that has been brushed and washed to raise the fibers for a fluffy, plush feel. The thick terry loops stay soft and absorbent over time.

Sew-through Button: A flat button with holes through which to sew onto the garment. Use on lightweight garments.

Shank Button: A button which has a loop on the back to provide space between itself and the garment. This shank enables fabric to pass through button and lay flat. This technique can be copied using sew-through buttons – simply create a shank by wrapping thread under the button.

Sharps: Sewing needle longer than quilting needles with a small eye; sizes 1-10.

Shrink: See pre-shrinking.

Shirring: Rows of machine gathering to take in fullness.

Shoulder Pads: Felt or foam shaped pads that are inserted into the shoulders of garments to give shape. Especially used in tailored garments and come in perform shapes and sizes.

Side Vents: Slits found at the bottom of side seams, used for fashion detailing, as well as comfort and ease of movement.

Side Seam: Side seam construction is the original, classic construction technique of t-shirt production. The tee is constructed with two large panels, for front and back sections. These panels are stitched together to ultimately form the torso covering. Sleeves and collars are then attached to finish the shirt.

Singles: A term used to indicate the diameter of a yarn. The smaller the number, the thicker the yarn.

Slash Pockets: A pocket in a garment to which access is provided by a vertical or diagonal slit in the outside of the garment.

Slip Stitch: A stitch used to turn under edges and to close gaps left for turning garments through. Stitches are barely visible on the right side.

Slit: An open part of a seam on a garment which is found on skirts.

Snips: Small cutting tool like scissors used to cut

thread.

Soft Shell: A fabrication that bonds an outer shell to a warm fleece or knit layer resulting in a breathable, flexible and comfortable jacket. All our soft shells have laminate for water resistance.

Soft Spun Cotton: Soft spun is an open-end yarn with more twist and a softer exterior to the yarn. The process generally helps lower torque and improve hand feel of the finished fabric.

Soft Wash: A specialty wash that gives these 100% ring spun combed cotton tees lighter-than-air softness and extra comfort.

Spandex: A manufactured elastometric fiber that can be repeatedly stretched over 500% without breaking and will still recover to its original length.

Sphere Dry: A patented fabric with a raised bumpy surface that lines the inside of the shirt, which not only creates an appealing athletic-inspired texture, but also works like a funnel to draw perspiration from the inside out. The fabric's three-dimensional construction also creates air space around the body to reduce cling.

Speciality Threads: These are threads used for embroidery that have a special effect. This can be metallic, neon, variegated, thicker woolen threads etc. Usually made from synthetic materials like rayons and metallics.

Speed Limiter: Sliding control located at the front of the machine that's used for limiting the sewing speed.

Spindle: The thread holder on a sewing machine. Also known as the thread Spool.

Spool: The thread holder on a sewing machine or a reel of thread. Also known as Spindle.

Stabilizer: Woven or non-woven material used beneath and hooped with the embroidered fabric to provide stability and support. These come in lots of different styles including fusible, soluble, tearaway and in various weights.

Stash: Collection of fabrics awaiting use!

Staystitching: This is a line of stitching done to stabilise fabric and prevent it from unwanted stretching prior to seaming. Usually done just inside the seam line on curved edges.

Stitch in the Ditch: This is a method of attaching facings or bias binding to the underside by stitching on the RIGHT side. Stitch in the seam by pulling fabric tight to left and right.

Stitch Length: Refers to the size of stitch. Most machines have a stitch length ranging from 0 to 5mm.

Stitch Width: Refers to the width of the zigzag and other stitches. Basic machines have a stitch width ranging from 0 to 5mm. Machines higher up the range have a width setting from 0 to 7mm. Some top-of-the-range models will go up to 9mm.

Straight Grain: This is what the grain line follows: the warp threads.

Straight Stitch: These are single forward stitches.

Stroking the Cat: Stitching in the direction of the grain (to find the direction of the grain, run finger along cut edge and stitch in direction in which fibers curl smoothly).

Stain Release: A fabric treatment that helps a garment release stains in the wash. Stain Repel. A fabric treatment that helps spills and stains easily roll off the garment.

Stonewashed: A process in which the fabric or garment is heavily washed with lava rocks or rubber/silicon balls, resulting in a softer fabric with a distressed, weathered look and reduced shrinkage.

Stop/Start Button: Found on most digital (computerized machines) gives the option to run the machine with the foot pedal disconnected. Sewing speed can then be easily controlled with the slider on the front of the machine. You can of course, use the variable speed foot pedal in the traditional way should you prefer.

Storm Flap: A piece of fabric that covers and protects an opening, usually a zipper, on an item of clothing. It is designed to add another barrier on more vulnerable parts of the clothing to protect against wind and moisture.

StormRepel®: A durable water-repellent (DWR) finish that sheds moisture so it doesn't soak in.

Straight Stitch: Normal stitch found on all sewing machines and is mainly used for sewing seams.

Stretch Stitch: Specially designed to sew stretchy, jersey fabrics. There are generally two types. Regular: used on light to medium weight stretch fabric. Triple: used for medium to heavier weight stretch fabrics. Most mechanical machines only have the triple stretch stitch. When sewing synthetic stretch, always use the special stretch needle to avoid skipped stitches.

Structured: A headwear term referring to a buckram lining used to control the slope of the cap.

Sublimation: A type of printing that uses sublimation ink, heat and pressure to transfer an image onto polyester fabric.

Sueded: A process in which fabric goes through a brushing process to raise the nap and give the garment a soft hand.

SEWING TERMS BEGINNING WITH

T

Tacking: See Basting.

Tailor's Tack: A way of marking placement points on garments for buttonholes, darts, pockets etc. A hand stitch, use a double length of thread to make two very loose loopy stitches through tissue pattern and both fabric layers. Snip the loops and pull fabric apart gently, snipping thread between layers so that some thread is in both fabric pieces. Always use a contrasting thread so Tailor's Tacks can be seen easily.

Take-up Lever: Part of the sewing mechanism that's located on the top left of the machine. Its purpose is to draw the top thread up from the fabric after the needle has formed the stitch with the bobbin thread. On nearly all modern machines, the take-up lever is either partially or totally hidden. Care must be taken to ensure this is correctly threaded (read the instruction book) otherwise thread jamming will definitely occur.

Taped Seams: A strip of fabric sewn to the seam of a garment to prevent distortion. In outerwear, taped seams aid in waterproofing.

Tapestry needle: Blunt needle with an eye that is long and oval; sizes 13-26.

Taslan: A durable and water repellent nylon fabric with a slightly shiny surface, used mainly in outerwear garments.

Teklon: A rugged, stronger Taslan nylon that is water repellent. Terra-TekTM Nylon. Durable and water repellent with a matte finish.

Tension: Tautness of the stitch which comes

from the pressure being exerted between the needle and bobbin. On a sewing machine there are two types of tension – thread and bobbin.

Tension Dial: Used for tightening or loosening the stitching.

Three Step Zigzag: Sometimes referred to as: multi zigzag, triple zigzag, trico stitch. Used for neatening seams, repairing tears in fabric and attaching elastic.

Thumbholes: Openings at the cuffs so they cover the back of the hands and the palms for warmth and enhanced fit.

Tie-Dye: A method of producing patterns by tying parts of the fabric to shield it from the dye.

Toile: This is a garment made from cheap fabric such as Calico and is used to 'prove' a pattern and to make sure the pattern fits perfectly. This is important to do when using expensive and delicate fabrics where alterations would mark like silk wedding dresses.

Top Load Bobbin: Aka drop-in bobbin.

Topstitching: A row of stitching that should be

visible on the finished garment. Top stitching can be decorative and/or functional as it also serves to hold facings in place.

Tracing Wheel: Used with carbon paper, it is a little serrated wheel that when rolled over the carbon paper, transfers the colour to fabric to mark placement lines for darts, pleats etc.

Tricot: A knit fabric of various natural or synthetic fibers like wool, silk, nylon or polyester having fine vertical ribs on the face and horizontal ribs on the back.

Tricot Lining: A very lightweight nylon lining often used in shorts.

Trim: Thin decorative strip such as ribbon or lace that is placed on a garment. This term is also used to describe cutting away excess fabric from seam allowances.

Triple-Needle Stitched: A finish commonly used on a sleeve or bottom hem that uses three needles to create parallel rows of visible stitching, giving the garment a cleaner, more finished look, as well as adding durability.

Tuck: A larger version of Pintuck – a fold in the

fabric that is stitched down.

Turn of the Cloth: This refers to the amount of fabric that is taken up in the fold when fabric is folded into two or turned through to right side. Particularly important to consider when dealing with bulky fabrics.

Tubular Collar: A collar knit in a tube form, so it has no seams.

Tuck-In Tails: A shirt constructed so the back hem is longer than the front. This aids in keeping the shirt tucked-in during normal activities.

Tuck Stitch: Refers to the look of the knit where some stitches are actually under the other stitches. Gives the shirt a waffle weave texture and look.

Tulip Hem: Two overlapping pieces of fabric at the hem of a garment which creates the look of a tulip petal.

Twill: A fabric characterized by micro diagonal ribs producing a soft, smooth finish. Commonly used for casual woven shirts.

Twill Tape: Attached to the inside of the placket

for a fashion effect.

Twin Needle: Special needle that will work on most modern sewing machines. It produces two parallel rows of stitching. They are available in a range of different widths: 1.6mm, 2mm, 3mm, 4mm and there's even a 6mm available for machines with a maximum stitch width of 7mm.

Two Ply: A yarn in which its thickness is made up of two layers or strands, adding durability and weight.

SEWING TERMS BEGINNING WITH

U

Underarm Grommets: Small holes in the armpit area to allow breathability and air circulation.

Underlining: Lining used to add body to a garment, placed between main fabric and interfacing. Also known as Interlining.

Understitching: A row of stitching through seam allowances and facings, very close to seam that attaches facing to main garment. Used to stop lining or facings from rolling out.

Universal Needle: A needle which has a slightly rounded tip. Used for woven and knit fabrics.

Universal Thread Tension: See Auto Tension

Unstructured: A headwear term referring to a low profile cap with a naturally low sloping crown. No buckram has been added to the crown for structure.

UV-Protective Fabric: A term used to refer to a fabric that resists the ability of ultraviolet rays to penetrate the fabric. Protects the fabric from fading and the wearer's skin from UV rays.

SEWING TERMS BEGINNING WITH

V

View: Found on paper patterns and refers to the variations in style of the garment.

V-Patch: A section of material in a V shape that is sewn onto a garment directly under the collar, providing support against stretching the neck opening. Also a style detail.

Vents: An opening in a garment which assists breathability and can aid in ease of decoration, allowing the garment to be hooped and embroidered with no visibility on the inside lining of the garment. Some vents are tacked down and are for fashion purposes only.

SEWING TERMS BEGINNING WITH

Wadding: Flat material used to stuff and pad, usually cotton, wool or fiberfill. (Also known as Batting).

Walking Foot: A presser foot for a sewing machine that allows even sewing over lots of layers or thicker fabric as it helps to grip the fabric layers and 'walks' it through when sewing. A menacing looking foot that is very useful!

Warp: Term describing the way the threads run lengthways through a woven fabric. Also known as 'lengthwise grain'.

Weft: Term describing the way the threads run at

right angles to the length of a woven fabric. Also known as 'cross grain'.

Welt: A method for covering raw edges of a pocket. This is the visible part of the binding on a buttonhole or pocket opening that looks like a lip.

Whipstitch: Strong over-edged hand stitch used for joining two edges together.

Wing Needle: A wide wing shaped needle which is flared at the sides to purposefully leave holes in fabric as it stitches. Use a wing needle on woven fabrics for heirloom stitching.

Wrong Side: This is the side of the fabric without the design – the side to be used as under or inside.

SEWING TERMS BEGINNING WITH

X

XY Axis: The directions an embroidery arm can move to pinpoint the correct location within the embroidery frame.

SEWING TERMS BEGINNING WITH

Y

Yarn Dyed: A term used when yarn is dyed prior to the weaving or knitting of the garment.

Yoke: A part of the garment fitted closely to the shoulders. Typically seen on the back as on a dress shirt, but may also be on the front, as on a Western style shirt.

SEWING TERMS BEGINNING WITH
Z

Zigzag Stitch: A stitch that goes diagonally side to side to produce a decorative finish to a seam or join two layers next to each other.

Zigzag Foot: General purpose foot that's supplied as standard with all sewing machines. Used mainly for straight or zigzag stitching.

Zip Foot: Specially designed presser foot that's used for inserting zips (not the concealed variety)

The needle sews on the outside edge of the foot enabling the stitching to get closer to the zip teeth.

Zipper Garage: A fold of soft fabric around the end of the zipper that helps prevent a scratched or irritated chin. Also known as a chin guard.

Useful links:
Embrocraft on Etsy:
https://www.etsy.com/uk/shop/Embrocraft

Embrocraft on Youtube:
https://www.youtube.com/channel/UC7GhMfk
dH5WJuGZFCM9FYLQ

Please note the YT channel is a work in progress and may not be completed until summer/autumn 2020.

MORE BOOKS BY TREV HUNT

Embroidery Machine Profits.

Embroidery Design Profits.
The Embrocraft A-Z of Fabric.
The Embrocraft A-Z of Embroidery.
The Embrocraft A-Z of Sewing.

ABOUT THE AUTHOR

Trev Hunt is the Author of five books about the sewing and embroidery industry.

Printed in Great Britain
by Amazon

48612087R00070